THIS IS A JOB FOR

MOMMY!

AN A-Z ADVENTURE

words by
Keegan
Connor Tracy

pictures by
Roz
MacLean

PROMONTORY
PRESS

THIS IS A JOB FOR MOMMY!

Promontory Press
www.promontorypress.com
ISBN: Paperback: 978-1-77374-016-4
Hardcover: 978-1-77374-027-0

Illustrations, Cover Design and Typeset by Roz MacLean

Printed in Canada

987654321

26 careers my mom has had
from A-Z they range.
It's okay to try out more than one
because life is full of change.

"THIS A JOB FOR MOMMY!"

is my happy cry,
because Mommy can do any job
and therefore, so can I!

Mommy started as an Actor,
she filmed in places near and far.
New York! Paris! Instanbul!
Even Cairo's Grand Bazaar!

Next she was a Baker,
who cooked up things so sweet.
If I ate up all my broccoli,
I'd get a gooey treat!

Then Mommy became a Cartographer,
she just loved geography.
She drew out maps of every place
you could visit by land or sea!

After that, she was a Diver,
she searched the seas for sunken ships.
She'd stay under water for hours
and hours,
making bubbles with her lips!

Then Mommy was an Engineer,
solving problems with her mind.
She taught me to make green energy
using a new, wind-powered turbine!

My mom became a Fisher next,
she was known for being bold!
She caught King Crab in Alaska
but decided it was just too cold!

Then she became a Geologist,
she studied sediment and rocks.
She could tell me what all the pebbles were
that showed up in my socks!

Herbalist was her next thing,
she learned how to heal with plants.
I loved to play in her big garden
and get tickled by the ants!

H

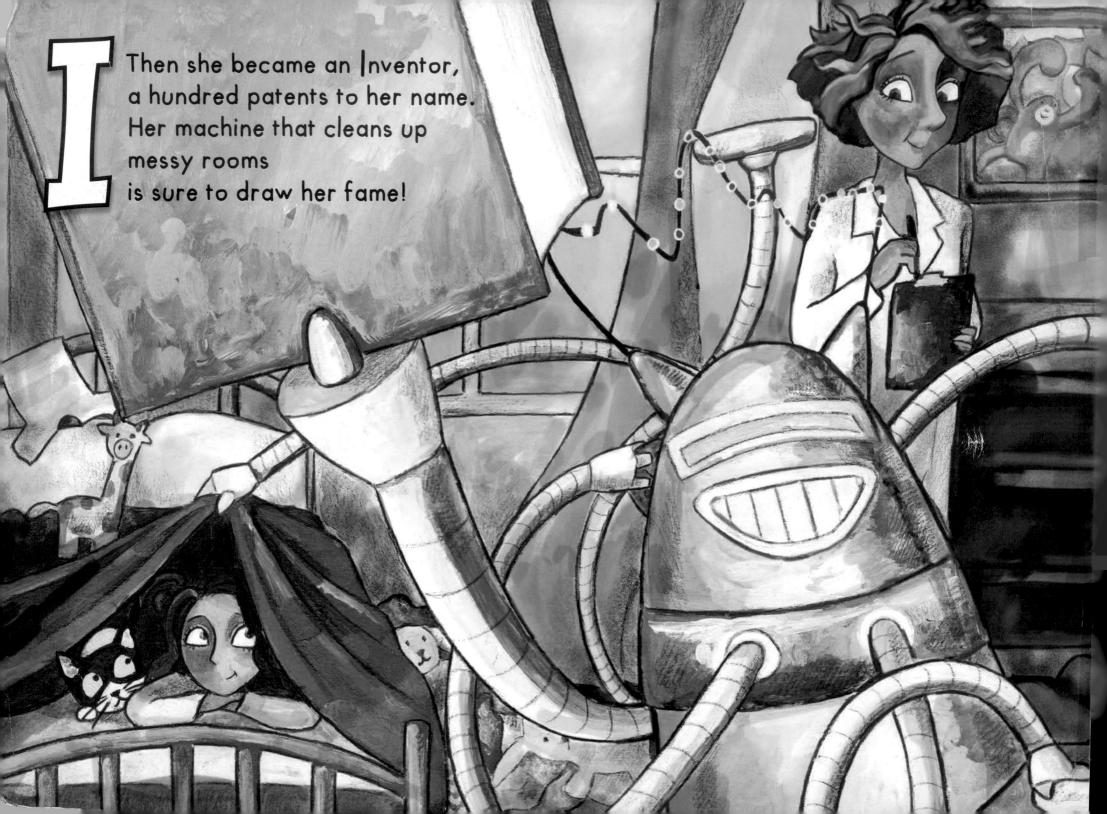

Then she became an Inventor,
a hundred patents to her name.
Her machine that cleans up
messy rooms
is sure to draw her fame!

After that she was a Journalist,
she loved to research and write.
Her best-loved piece was the history
of Van Gogh's 'Starry Night'!

J

But Mommy loved adventure,
so she became a Kayak Pro!
She says in life and in the rapids,
it's best to just go with the flow!

Then Mommy became a Lifeguard,
her swimming was so strong!
She was always there at water's edge
in case anything went wrong!

Mommy next became a Miner,
going deep, deep underground.
Digging coal and rocks and minerals
'til no more could be found!

After that she was an Oboist,
in a world-famous symphony.
She played Mozart, Bach, and Brahms,
and songs written just for me!

After that, a Police Detective,
sometimes in disguise!
She would often ask the questions
that would put away bad guys!

Next she was a Rodeo Clown,
her costume crimson red.
She stopped that job after one mad bull
tossed her right onto her head!

R

Then she was a Stuntwoman,
no building was too tall!
She was attached to special cables
so she'd be safe in every fall!

My mom became a
Teacher next,
she taught woodworking
and shop.

Her class built an Eiffel Tower
and I couldn't even reach
the top!

T

After that, a Ufologist,
she studied UFOs!
She says she believes in aliens,
but that no one really knows . . .

Next, she was a Ventriloquist
Vaudeville was her inspiration.
She and her funny puppet
sold out shows across the nation!

After that a Window Washer,
'cause she's the bravest mom alive.
She never was afraid of heights,
even on floor ninety-five!

Then Mommy became an X-ray Tech,
snapping pictures of folks' insides.
An x-ray can see everything,
There's nowhere inside to hide!

Then my mom became a Yogi,
she could do any yoga pose.
She was so lithe and limber
she touched her forehead with her toes!

Now Mommy's a Zoologist
spending her days with chimpanzees.
We rescue injured animals
under jungle canopies!

Z

All mommies are amazing, whatever jobs they do.

They show us all by doing them that we could do them too!

the end.

Keegan Connor Tracy is an award winning actress from Vancouver. She was inspired to write this book after thinking about all the interesting careers she's had on TV and in movies. What makes her happiest is using her imagination - as a writer, as a filmmaker and as a storyteller. She hopes this book makes you wonder what you could be!?

Roz MacLean is an award winning author / illustrator and educator from Vancouver, BC. Previous picture books she has written and illustrated include "The Body Book," and "Violet's Cloudy Day." She loves how books and pictures can help readers to see the beauty in difference and the possibilities of our imaginations.